HAUNTED SHIPS, PLANES, and CARS

Grace Ramsey

Rourke
Educational Media

rourkeeducationalmedia.com

Guided Reading Level: Q

Scan for Related Titles
and Teacher Resources

Table of Contents

Haunted Travels.. 4

Ghost Ships 7

Spooky Skies 14

Sinister Cars 21

Studying the Paranormal 29

Index 31

Show What You Know.................................. 31

About the Author 32

Haunted Travels

A ship appears on the horizon, then vanishes. A man in a pilot's uniform speaks to an airline's crew moments before takeoff. Then he disappears.

An ordinary car turns into a killing machine—that seemingly
can't be destroyed.

5

Ships, planes, and cars are used to **transport** people and cargo every day. There is nothing unusual about most of them. But when strange things happen, some people think, "Yikes! It's haunted!"

Ghost Ships

Reports of ghost ships are sprinkled throughout history. These aren't regular ships filled with spirits, though. The entire vessel is said to be a **phantom**.

Paranormal research involves looking for evidence of supernatural activity, such as ghosts and hauntings. This type of activity is not explained by science or the laws of nature.

In 1748, the *Lady Lovibond* set sail to celebrate the ship captain's wedding. But not all on board were happy about the union. A jealous man steered the ship into a sandbank off the coast of England. The ship sank, killing everyone on board.

Since then, the ship is said to be spotted every 50 years, sailing around the coast. Some **witnesses** think it's in distress. They send out rescuers, but the ship cannot be found.

The *Palatine Light* is one of the most famous American ghost ship legends. Witnesses say the 18th century ship lights up the night near Rhode Island's Block Island. The sightings only happen during the week between Christmas and New Year's Day.

There is no record of a ship called *Palatine* wrecking in the area. Historians think the sightings may be tied to the wreck of the *Princess Augusta* in 1738. When the ship ran aground near Block Island, many of the passengers and crew were sick or dead from fever. The captain refused to let the sick go ashore.

The world's most famous ghost ship tale is that of *The Flying Dutchman*. The legend began in 1641 when a Dutch ship ran into fierce storms off the coast of the Cape of Good Hope.

The ship's crew battled to get out of the storm. As the ship began to sink, the captain screamed a curse. He **vowed** to sail until doomsday.

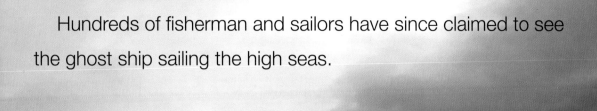

Hundreds of fisherman and sailors have since claimed to see the ghost ship sailing the high seas.

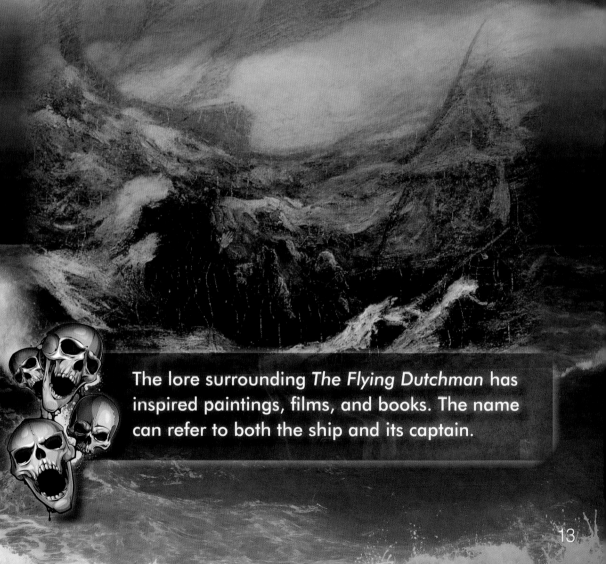

The lore surrounding *The Flying Dutchman* has inspired paintings, films, and books. The name can refer to both the ship and its captain.

Spooky Skies

Shipwrecks aren't the only disasters that lead to haunting tales. Plane tragedies also have their own spirited stories.

During the filming of *Casino Royale*, the movie crew refused to board a 30-year-old plane used for some scenes. Why? Because it was haunted! The jet had no power, but lights would go on and off. Some claimed to see a woman gliding through the aisle. It's said this woman died of a heart attack on board years before.

In 1977, two planes collided on a runway in Tenerife, Spain, killing 583 people. Now, some say the spirits of the victims haunt the tarmac. They appear in large numbers, waving frantically at the planes awaiting takeoff.

A warning, perhaps, of possible danger.

In 1979, American Airlines Flight 191 crashed shortly after takeoff at Chicago's O'Hare Airport. The crash killed 270 people on board and two on the ground.

The crash of Flight 191 is among the worst plane crashes in American history.

Some nearby residents say the spirits of passengers have knocked on their doors, looking for their luggage.

The wreckage was cleared long ago, but the crash site was never the same. Witnesses say the temperature drops noticeably, followed by the sounds of screams from the empty field. Drivers on nearby roads report seeing strange lights and ghostly figures.

Eastern Airlines Flight 401 plummeted into the Florida Everglades in 1972. The tragedy killed 101 people, including the pilot and flight engineer. But these men weren't done flying.

Parts of the wrecked plane were salvaged and fitted on other aircraft. That's when flight crews started seeing these dedicated spirits on board. The apparitions were so well-defined, people didn't think anything of their presence.

Until the men disappeared before their eyes.

A flight captain and two flight attendants say they spoke to one of the pilots before take-off, unaware of anything unusual. Then, they watched him vanish. They were so shaken, they canceled the flight.

Singapore Airlines has had its own fleet of haunted jets. According to reports, crew members were petrified when assigned to a few of the airline's 747s. Angry ghosts were said to stalk the aisles, sometimes throwing silverware.

Sinister Cars

Like planes, sometimes wrecked cars are salvaged for usable parts. Sometimes those parts seem to be bad luck, at best. Some say they are cursed.

Movie star James Dean was excited about his new Porsche 550 Spyder. But a friend told him to get rid of it, or he would be dead in a week. The man got a **sinister** feeling from the car. Dean's girlfriend refused to get in it. Others warned him, as well, according to the legend of the "Death Car."

A week later, Dean died in a head-on collision.

Parts of the mangled Spyder were installed in another race car. The driver hit a tree and died instantly.

Dean's wrecked car was stored in a garage at one time. The garage caught fire, burning to the ground. The car was untouched by the flames.

U.S. President John F. Kennedy (1917-1963) was assassinated in his 1961 Lincoln 74A convertible on a November afternoon. The car was modified and kept in service after his death, until it was retired to the Henry Ford Museum in 1978.

An apparition is said to appear near the car, especially in November.

Archduke Franz Ferdinand of Austria (1863-1914) and his wife were shot by an assassin as they sat in their limousine. The archduke's death launched World War I.

Archduke Franz Ferdinand and his wife, Sophie, shortly before they were killed.

Over the next 20 years, the limo was owned by fifteen people. It was involved in six accidents and thirteen deaths. Some say the vehicle is cursed.

The archduke's killer limousine is now on display at the War History Museum of Vienna.

What turns something ordinary like a car or plane into something spooky? Some think spirits can attach themselves to objects that were part of their death.

Some think it's possible for unhuman **entities**, such as demons, to attach themselves to ordinary objects.

Many paranormal researchers are interested in proving whether a spirit can, in fact, attach to an object.

Some people think ghost ships **manifest** from the energy left behind by tragic shipwrecks.

Traumatic events are thought to leave imprints on a location. Some say these imprints play over and over, like a movie on repeat.

Skeptics say ghost ships are simply mirages. They think ghost sightings are people's minds playing tricks on them. Can ships, planes, and cars really be haunted?

What do you believe?

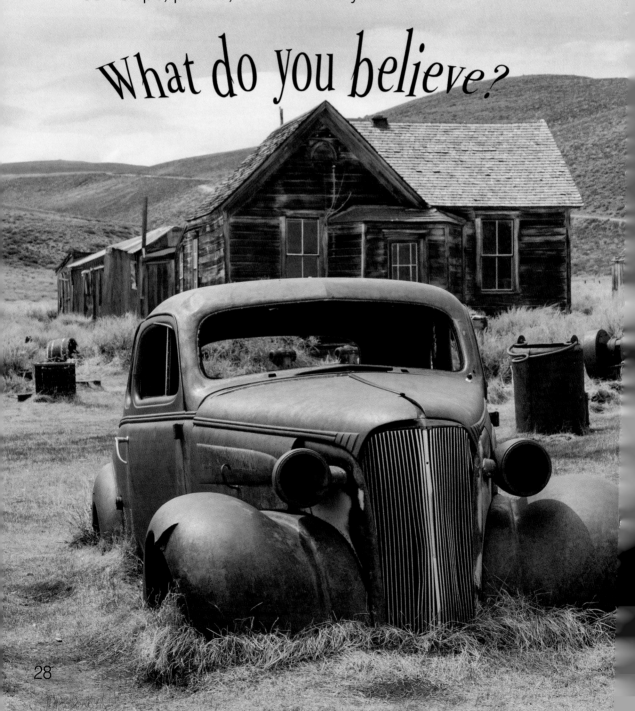

Studying the Paranormal

Paranormal researchers aren't just after spooky thrills. The purpose of investigations is to capture evidence that can help further our understanding of supernatural phenomena.

These investigations are also done sometimes to give peace of mind to someone who thinks they are being haunted.

A good researcher will always look for a natural explanation first when investigating a reported haunting.

Want to learn more about hauntings, and the tools and methods paranormal investigators use?

Check out these websites:

http://kids.ghostvillage.com

www.scaryforkids.com/true-stories

www.paranormalghost.com/ghost_hunter_101.htm

Glossary

entities (IN-tuh-tees): things with distinct and independent existences

manifest (MAN-uh-fest): display or show by one's acts or appearance

paranormal (PAR-uh-nor-muhl): events or phenomena that are beyond the scope of normal scientific understanding

phantom (FAN-tuhm): a ghost

skeptics (SKEP-ticks): people who doubt the truth or validity of a claim or belief

sinister (SIN-iss-tuhr): giving the impression that something harmful or evil is happening or will happen

transport (tran-SPORT): take or carry people or goods from one place to another

vowed (vowd): solemnly promised to do a specified thing

witnesses (WIT-nis-ehs): people who see an event, typically a crime or accident, take place

Index

Dean, James 22, 23

Ferdinand, Franz 25

Flight 191 16, 17

Flight 401 18, 19

Flying Dutchman, The 12, 13

Kennedy, John F. 24

Lady Lovibond 8, 9

O'Hare Airport 16, 17

Palatine Light 10

Show What You Know

1. Why might a traumatic event lead to a haunting?

2. What might a skeptic think causes people to believe in hauntings?

3. Why did people warn James Dean about driving his new car?

4. Why do you think people are inspired to create art and stories about The Flying Dutchman?

5. Why might the airline pilot and engineer of Flight 401 still appear to people on planes?

About the Author

Grace Ramsey is a journalist, author, and mega-fan of paranormal research shows. She once joined a crew of investigators at one of the world's most haunted places. Her experiences there made her much less skeptical of the supernatural. She still gets the chills just thinking about that night. Yikes!

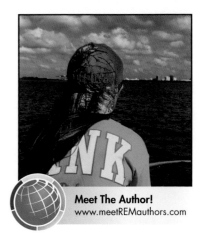

Meet The Author!
www.meetREMauthors.com

© 2017 Rourke Educational Media

www.rourkeeducationalmedia.com

Though there has been plenty of research done by believers and skeptics alike, there is no definitive scientific proof that ghosts are real. This series explores the stories of hauntings as told by those who claim to have experienced them. The publisher and authors do not endorse any claims herein as fact.

PHOTO CREDITS: Cover/Title Page © Predrag Vuckovic; Page 4-5 © Krittanum Panpetch 0873157126; Page 6 © RickTravel; Page 7 © breakermaximus; Page 8 © Heartland-Arts; Page 9 © Steven van Soldt; Page 10-11 © lenarts; Page 12 © sylphe_7; Page 13 © Albert Pinkham Ryder/Wikipedia; Page 14 © Andrew Penner; Page 15 © Kativ; Page 16 © Visions of America; Page 17 © EdBockStock; Page 18-19 © John Proctor/Wikipedia; Page 20 © baona; Page 21 © Nick Starichenko; Page 22 © AF archive/Alamy Stock Photo; Page 23 © Pictorial Press Ltd/Alamy Stock Photo; Page 24 © Ian Dagnall/Alamy Stock Photo; Page 25 © Karl Tröstl/ Europeana/Wikipedia, Alexf; Page 26 © vicnt; Page 27 © Angelo Gianpiccolo; Page 28 © photoquest; Page 29 © Ratstuben

Edited by: Keli Sipperley
Cover and interior design by: Jen Thomas

Library of Congress PCN Data

Haunted Ships, Planes, and Cars/Grace Ramsey
(Yikes! It's Haunted)
ISBN (hard cover)(alk. paper) 978-1-68191-764-1
ISBN (soft cover) 978-1-68191-865-5
ISBN (e-Book) 978-1-68191-954-6
Library of Congress Control Number: 2016932725

Also Available as:

ROURKE'S
e-Books